RENEWALS 691-4574

DATE DUE

MAY 1 0			
GAYLORD			PRINTED IN U.S.A.

Black Holes,
Black Stockings

Wesleyan Poetry

Black Holes,
Black Stockings

Olga Broumas
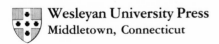
Jane Miller

Wesleyan University Press
Middletown, Connecticut

Some of the untitled poems in this book appeared originally in these magazines: *No Apologies*, "If I'm introduced wearing indigo toenail polish. . . . ," "While she showered we listened to her practice-tape. . . ." "The best jump lightly into the air and lift more lightly. . . ."; *Womantide*, "She liked to be in the middle. . . ." "I alter nothing for her. . . ."

The lines beginning "periplum, / not as land looks on a map / but as sea bord seen by men sailing" are reprinted from "The Pisan Cantos LIX" in *The Cantos of Ezra Pound*, Copyright 1940 by Ezra Pound. Reprinted by permission of New Directions Publishing Corporation and Faber and Faber Ltd.

The lines beginning "Do not come back. If you can bear it, be . . . / as the farthest sometimes helps: in me" from "Requiem for a Friend" in *Rilke: Between Roots. Selected Poems Rendered from the German* by Rika Lesser. To be published by Princeton University Press.

Library of Congress Cataloging in Publication Data

Broumas, Olga, 1949-
    Black holes, black stockings.

(Wesleyan Poetry)

    I. Miller, Jane, 1949- . II. Title.
PS3552.R6819B58   1985   811'.54   85-7128
ISBN 0-8195-5141-4 (cloth: alk. paper)
ISBN 0-8195-6141-X (pbk.: alk. paper)

All inquiries and permissions requests should be addressed to the Publisher, Wesleyan University Press, 110 Mt. Vernon Street, Middletown, Connecticut 06457

Distributed by Harper & Row Publishers, Keystone Industrial Park, Scranton, Pennsylvania 18512.

Manufactured in the United States of America

First Edition

Wesleyan Poetry

We thank the John Simon Guggenheim Memorial Foundation for its support;

Doris and Sotiri Haralambidi and Hélène Sauret for their generous hospitality.

Black Holes,
Black Stockings

Enfleurage

As from a water lily, *periplum,*

not as land looks on a map
        but as sea bord seen by men sailing
successive ferries, my toy boats, leaf, song, heart. Or again, I step
into a street and, commensurate with its width its bazaar breaks
into range, wares, voices, steam float distinctly in unequal units
closer. A blur of relations and then synchromesh: rachet, whistle,
bulk, cold, scallion bitter, fish heads, city dock. Out of the midst
of the city the country, forested one by one into many, alert like
the tops of trees with inexact news about an imminent arrival; I
tilt until it becomes time and there she is, most beautiful come
upon from behind, where she is waiting for a moment, discour-
aged her message never arrived. And as she turns, her sunglasses
glint and she brushes back her braid where her hair was loose
before, and since; there is no one of them that does not see her,
unconsciously—and, white birds casting a dark shadow, fly out
of themselves.

We parked and hiked and climbed over the wide sleeve of the Atlantic. Below and between, the beach where even in season the many travelers rested or tossed far apart. In perfect September I sent them to be alone. Without mission or admonition. Feeling as we did then about each other, already relaxed, how would two wed the fall of summer, speechless for three days, how far from the other? Satin shorts and roller skates at night in the streets of the village, transvestites. Perrier and pistachio. The fabulous dark divulging day, deliberately provoked. Saran wrap and plexiglass about the night and the day, the membrane between them. I thought we might lap and here at the great magnet meet. I unmade my bed, wind torn from clouds, massaged by distance, and slept. We pull on cords from the earth where we are joined. We the plural.

She liked to be in the middle. One of them was taken by how close her heart beat to the surface like a robin's and how she landed with a light touch. If the sheets were white and the sun glanced on them, blond had more red. Another was olive with almond eyes, who liked to wake slowly and fall back. She lay beside the row of windows and rolled out into the night on their long wooden oven spoons. Sometimes they came for her and woke her, kissing the corners of her mouth. The long hairs in the bed, the very curly, the weighty and the subtle, lit an arabesque. When they were wet they were very very wet, and when they were dry they were funny. Excited, the candle burned like cry-breath. Who called out and where answered and when became thirsty. She reached for the lucky pitcher sailing across the sky. Tissue, tissue, kiss you.

She didn't think we were married in any traditional sense so didn't hesitate to apply first to one and then the other the awkward silences which her colorful beauty could be felt to fill, as in panavision, setting a slower mood for the spectator perhaps but quickening her pulse. *Don't leave*, she didn't whisper, nor *stay with me*, but rather shifted her hair as one shifts an entire pose left to right close-up, taking a minute, triggering the free association where every promise lost or denied finds its place. Blue skies, tawny beach, sea-green and berry stain. By year's end she would bring us one of her first architecture assignments, in the manner of the Japanese masters, the arrangement of dots in disorder. Impressionable and expressive, she lined the corridors with butcher paper, unable to avoid herself and, hence, design— wool-bodies, lace, the infinite destinies of flakes, ceramic poros- ity, wormwood. She would hide sea, sand and boat by hanging the sheet upside down. Told to watch water boil, stray rain, to unre- hearse them, she did it many times and in her mind, until by ear first fathomed disarray.

the only cool day of summer
kids at bullfights
yellow and purple
green olives under an almond tree
a trapezoid smile
indoors without a flash
two aunts and an uncle
avocado vinaigrette
a bath with no hot water
a spoon and a fork
illuminated hands of a clock on its side
the hidden side of an arriving train
Paris at night
a face appearing at different windows of a big house
the last half of April and the first of May
one other

Like shower over the heart muscle and, after rain, summer. Peaches and rose. A steam bath for the earth, Chinese massage, long silver pins drawn the great distance of daylight from hand-clouds into trees standing on their heads, roots. Waterwheel over the terraced vertebrae, earthface rosé tanning toward the many the long the most generous hours of light that today rain, yet light, the lightest gray, gray apple-green, gray lilac, white. Solstice of pins, of verticals, into the haunches of horsehills. Tongues in puddles. Hours in twos and threes, hours in elongated seconds, thick sentences taut and thinning into words and finally breaking into alphabet, moments without shadow, the long spaces between lights in a countryside going to sleep in even daylight from the rain, and the different lamps meeting in the evening making gold the gray, buttering the houses in small swatches as if they were children holding out their pieces of bread, watching the last light perforate the darkness and not admit to it, no it shall never, happy soul, winter.

Round Sunday. Wooded plains underwater, seaweed, urchin, sea-horse, and the gelatinous os implanted on the rock. Its rose madder flowered—the myth of the toothed—a sunrise of tresses to cilialike ease in its prey. The rose flash sweeps the waterwind. And when the mouth puckers, cordovan, doorless, it confounds. Smoke-moon enamel from a distance, traversed by speedboat the sea jells into membrane, petrol green on descent. We thought silverfish until the boat stopped and we saw seaweed reflected as silver-leafed poplars. Cricket island. White flowers of summer like winter, milksnake feeding on the paproot. Nimble light we crack diving. The horn of the troubadour is forced outside the self in shape, where we bob a brief note in the after-dive. Allowing someone else to panic where I was playing, taking the whole hillside for a friend from far asea, the sea grapes, emptying its vacuum of charged bubbles from a double-prowed cruiser, both wakes. Day necklace, night glass unwobbling. The first inch is forgiveness. The noun that is cleaned disappears. Putting up with their manifestations like smoke in our faces already turned from that elegant perfume, like flamingos who wandered north from the tropics, we concentrate on abiding. Our body casts out a cypress root as logos while the unharnessed gray whale escapes the muffle of the ocean wash: fattest cows and youngest heifers, beautiful electronic images, the loneliness of their small good hearts. All the nights go on by hand, journey of a thousand knots, milk again learning nothing. Ha! Priests! Red lamp poles, muscadet sky: upside down. Parakeets in the afterlife, silverpious, pass to slope the world. Pre-Alps, perched villages, memories, as when you fall asleep god exists. Some visible keeping still, opium, oyster, the unswirling of the smoke unswirling the mollusk, signals us to daily with the frail. The sound of a nut opening, brain-wake.

Since I dreamt of a lion with a cat on its back, the tear which is glass which is stone in a ring in its eye, I lay on the beach dimly and therefore elementally, taking the pearl from her mouth back into the mussel, irregular, tearlike, breaking it down. Dissolve the pearl and remove the irritant carefully to the sea floor where the crystalline, faceted, rocks and fits. The whole bar shifting clouds in the water. Deeper, a sun-ray shower plummets to a plateau below which, unirradiated, free-form masses of water tilt and lug to the basalt and its schism, oiling their sides with black molt oozing from crusted chimneys, cellar fire. Fantastically weeps the eye of fire.

A gram. How much?
Are you married?
Yes.
Is she?
Of course.
Where are your men?
My husband is arriving later.
Will he let you go?
Of course. Where are we going?
I will meet you here at 4 o'clock.
How much?
He will let you go?
4 o'clock.

Blue of rainforest green, of moss, ultamarine of closed eyes, evening pearl, berry black, blue of earth cerulean in space, royal, prussian; porpoise blue and whale gray, slate blue of metal, enamel; iridescent trout, blue of fungus and mold; sky, pacific, mediterranean, aqua of translucent blues, blue stained with yellow; iris, silver, purple, rose blue, military, grape; in the shadow, violet or port; pool blue, quivering; church-stain, red madder, octopal; ice blue; blue of sighs, bluebird in twilight with a white stripe; polka dot, blood blue, nordic, light; diamond, meteor; parallel lines, density; powder, red, white and blue, blue concerto, island.

Second Epitaph

On the somber banks of Mélas, in Tamassos of Pamphylia,
I, daughter of Damophylos, Bilitis, was born. I rest far
from my country, you can see.

Very young I learned the loves of Adonis and Astarte,
the mysteries of the Syrian saint, and the death and return
toward Her-of-the-round-eyelids.

If I was courtesan, what's to blame? Wasn't that my
female duty? Stranger, the mother of all things guides us.
Not to have gratitude isn't prudent.

In gratitude to you who have stopped, I wish you this
destiny: may you be loved, not love. Good-bye. Remember in
your old age that you have seen my tomb.

She rose from them, walked through the room, at the door bowed, and turned. It was her opportunity between formal good-bye and exit to judge the impression she had made, a demilitarized zone in which she was already assumed gone. Bowing, she kept her eyes up to fix the panorama and trick an accidental gaze into a matching bow. Taken by surprise and politeness, invariably he smiled into her closing eyes, eroticized, in her favor, where she left him. She had been presented by the minor official but it was the general with whom she had slept a month ago and to whom she had addressed her request, without looking at him in either case, the latter according to his preference, the former hers, as in wearing her hair severely back and off her neck—having discovered in a similarly critical situation with a gentleman of means that one is seen and not recognized if a great feature like the hair is hidden. And turned in her handwoven silk scarf embossed with an ancient script without a word, having chosen the few necessary ones which had been repeated twice, once for the general, in the straightforward manner he had asked her once for a certain act, and the second time that the general's audience might take in her beautiful white skin where the royal blue kimono cut away. An ivory sash swung at the slit if she gestured, which she reserved for when things were going well; they had. Her lover would be released from prison where he had been detained five months earlier for contraband and was sick from claustrophobia and filth. She had been allowed to visit him and was given a handmade Malay suit as she had been given her impeccable manner: from the poor, who accepted her generosity of spirit—and money when she had it—returning abundantly like the beloved silkworm.

To Gyrinno

Don't believe that I have loved you. I ate you like a berry fig, I drank you like ardent water, I carried you around me like a clasp of skin.

I amused myself with your body because you have short hair, pointed breasts on your thin body, and black nipples like two small dates.

As fruit needs water, a woman also is necessary, but already I no longer know your name, you who have passed through my arms like the shadow of another adored.

Between your skin and mine, a burning dream possessed me. I threw you on me as on a wound and I cried Mnasidika! Mnasidika! Mnasidika!

There's a song of privacy that begins Go away Go away, and stills the mice and the porcupine too, crouched at the door as you fiddle the keyhole. Lizards, asleep, roll a little farther from your bed, spiders hand over hand in the moonlight climb as if to it, holding the rim of the amber pot until a signal to scale down again. Alone, alone, the sweet golden beads with their interior lights guided by destiny guiding night travelers beyond, back or askew into the not-here, the knot in the crossroads where they must tire and halt like a girl caught in her hair where the teeth of the combs are too tight together, throwing the comb down and sleeping deeply on the tangle, worsening it, happy in dream. Tomorrow it will be snipped away, tomorrow the porcupine will startle you from the fig tree, pointing its tears at you or, worse, beyond to some backfire or allergen thriving among the geraniums; snag, broken egg, broken string. But now the silent choral, the poppy growing sunflower-size in a vibration Chagallesque, tipped in flare burning in, tranquil candelabra with its funny rhyme glowing inside you.

Lizards and ants yes, mosquitos and flies no. Yellowjackets yes, wasps gnats bumblebees no. Nightingales, swallows, woodchucks, dragonflies, fireflies yes. Mina birds usually. Kittens, puppies, guppies; pigeons, doves, yes. Owls, not usually. Nor do I like dogs in packs or frog-singing, mating in the fog with his camouflaged baritone. Buggers. Do flies bite? One mother is a bitch and the other pink and pert. They were here for a performance and tea, mothers of famous lovers. Serum is squeezed out of a bite, not without pain but the itch is gone; makes a funny mark where you've bleached your leg hair rather than shave. We all sang Try A Little Tenderness. Risk of pus. The countess invited her publisher and one mother a series of relatives. Split genes, clones, insomniacs, reptiles no. Fly-by-night, tea-for-two. One sang for mother, another recited. Goods for nothing, good for nothings: one loves two who loves three. I took each Polaroid into the sun: the countess and mother-in-mourning are dark against the great blue; the other mother and the countess again, impressionistic, fleeting; a third, of the four of them: daughters and mothers who had been—over-exposed in front of a bowl of wild strawberries bleeding together a little. Looking up I saw out of place on a fig tree limb a rather large mouse staring down the fabulous blouses of great beauties with a secret, mine, happy no matter, pulling it off. We spent the last hour of the night, at last, just looking at each other alone.

If I'm introduced wearing indigo toenail polish, my favorite by Stendhal, she will never imagine me her daughter's lover. Like the hotel girl, wide-eyed we would accept a *letto matrimoniale* just to be sea-side. She was fifteen, indifferent to the sea, a sexy flounce to her pinafore over the slight maillot. She too admired my nails, in the elevator.

While she showered we listened to her practice-tape and sang. My pelvic bone was sore. I cut garlic for spinach. Meanwhile the countess had sent her Russian editor to ask about our armchair, whether it was blue-green or green-blue, to see what we were doing. We had not been to her tea and would not be at her sheep roast. She was told we weren't dressed. It was four in the afternoon, the first of June, geraniums opening for their second and lovelier bloom, ants coursing the porch in the blindspot of a lizard's amphiopia. I stepped on the head of a nail lying on its side as I mocked the countess; she was formidable. All day released its minutes and hours like someone in a park throwing feed, a little here and there, more where we made love. Many times that week the wind had blown a door shut, a tray over, a curtain; diminished now to sailing a few petals across a bowl of water. She would leave again—this time without ceremony, either at the countess's or by waving down a premature train—slowly north and then dramatically south; we would make exchanges with the night, petals ourselves, still where we unburden, quivering to receive. Knowing its completion is return, one says good-bye confidently; the other gets in the car with me.

To have by heart a complexity beyond mind's intervention, I lay a curtain over the bird-cage brain, open to the close world of the ant, how it scurries with its meal the size of its head! O improportion, towel mountaining the surface of the hot porch the insect must traverse, especially as I step, making out of a foot a black cloud out of a blue sky, the sudden dark of one of you going away, going away. Followed, fallow, fuel, we are star between earth and nothing blond graying into white. In the background someone is always knocking hard on the door wanting in, unable to imagine what takes so long, who goes so far, which one of them, a triptych in the Chinese vein where seasons are simultaneous. There was no name for it, pair and odd, pair and odd, or did I dream you there, song of my region? The words anybody can use them, ΣΤΗΝ ΑΚΡΗ ΤΟΥ ΣΥΛΛΟΓΙΣΜΟΥ ΠΑΡΑΜΕΡΑ ΜΙΑ ΛΕΞΗ, turned on their heads side to side. Pigeons like roving seashells on the quai talking as fast as a Parisian. The caption-making intellect among the floral postal cards, a vaseful in the city, a season in Provence.

The felicitous four-leaf clover appears in the lavender fields; hears and is the nut. Or at least one left, returned; at last forgiving the nostalgias. The past is any one. Without your will but for luck different. In front even we know the rest. Thus on the lip of things already evening is here, serene, or in photograph where the wind arranges embraces. A transparency such that you keep on seeing the human arriving. And the fear of love feeling with its hands on top of ghosts, many-passionate and invisible, gilded, they have their traps. Not revealed we feel. Calmly the sunset anchors. We say before the summer is over we understand the tiles are jewels, even though in full moon they become swinging doors moment after moment. Time is practice. Before, during, after, east one mile, waves, weeds, right and left, the third one, almost, best, worst, continuous, aside. One chooses to pick up. But there with two silences, especially then it seems, also from far away, is a drop rubbed between the fingers, dark, speaking in the singular. Perhaps only the night and day, little churches, nothing we know. Like something broke from you. You see now, coffee-colored, so strong, from top to bottom like a mirror. How beautiful power, as a girl without suspicion and tonight dressed with a pot of basil, remains. All this sun and trees, homeland with French sky. The birds even come down without reason, light. A body twice with lightning as when saints are children, blue beads, understanding, sounds, halves. But tied, untied, given a laurel among the trees who knew you, we loved this side of our names like this side of August and this island. July flew on its silvering becoming night all the way to catch morning, jumping into other sky and pawning its ring. *Now*, hurrying. Decorated in yellow braid with an artificial rose, ravenous, it became younger and younger to us. And from under its covering of black grapes finished smoking its cigarette, erotic, perfumed, to sit opposite us, then upon us. Behind the smoke set the red sky like a fresco. Who can guess what it means? The previous day, the broken violets, quiet, and the Saturdays combing their hair away from the part—all put their heads out for good-byes. The voluptuous sorrows are aired like big sunflowers before rain, and the too many mistakes and the repetitions overdoing their promises have eaten too much. Love, joy, ten rosy thresholds only recently deserted and always about to be, terrifying fadings in and out, hands beckoning and finding the beginning in the east cheer the newcomer. But the groundswell so soft while we are only standing only enjoying the wind is already aware of the strange dark with white teeth that will drink and in clouds and incense force a move. The first pebbles slide, the tethers prickle. Momentary sanctuary like the spray of thyme and benjamin. Unimaginings like climbers descending, experience disordering, healings with a little blood on them, these widows of magnificence marry again, marrying us.

Your aunt's daughter married a diplomat, the perfect setting for her having been raised in several languages. The children now added Spanish and Portuguese to the list, and spoke these to each other at the dinner table, gliding their feminine endings under the Arabic and French. I was remembering how a left-handed person ought to manage the fish knife beside the easeful manners of the children. The German asked about my work and his children followed my English, the language they liked least. We thought about being sorry for not having changed our day-clothes, not when they asked their daughter to curtsy but when she did it and remained mercilessly untouched. We thought it would ease her release later for her mother to have excused our freedom, thinking the important fact would have been that we knew how to dress with our money, like her. We saw the snapshots of Buenos Aires and heard about having to hide the Mercedes and use the old car; not stepping out at night—that they had to be fortressed he saw as a mark of distinction, as he said with some pleasure. Everyone ruffled at the table except the aunt, who was loved, and whose reasons for being pleased that we had brought flowers were insignificant beside the first one—they were simply beautiful.

She brought her sister to the stone house and they filled the room with an Egyptian smokiness, unfiltered and slow burning, like the light on their childhood beaches, desert completely to the water, and the rain that had brought them inside parted with the mistral, then only in its infancy but already brushing the wicker chairs a few feet across the stones and their hair across the chords. The following day it would clear the sky and break a glass on one of them, a pâté knife asleep on a plate of food, as they lay on the stones of the patio, blowsy with their success.

She struck the tuning fork and pressed the ball at its tip to her teeth—oral and aural cavity resounding the pure A, cranial cavity flushed—such an intimate gesture where their nakedness had been as casual as the magnetic tape's cling to a limb's neutral magnetic skin. August above the bowery, windows shut against traffic—the synthesizer, shower, and the famous bed thinned from its opulence in novels, in the graphite above its head, a fat cotton mat between the swivel speakers on the floor. On it the instruments during the day rotated, on it the comrade nights, carbonite wind east-west across the loft, damp and possessive. Showering every hour while they taped, they still easily knew one was wet, where it dried slower than water on the leather stools, one dry. They didn't dress for intruders, nor did they act out rumors, not without lapse, awkward or as in the moment when, broken from the keyboards and the amp by deep contraction, they embraced, dissimulating, diverged into strangers by fantasy, replaced by full sexual subject, rapacious, afraid. They kissed and smoothed each other's shoulderblades, where wings had prepared to fly.

Of those we have let go—those shy to scandal, those of your country unwilling to forgive your exile, the almost-as-famous, the nostalgic, those who accelerate scandal, those willing to forgive, who hold to blame as to a leash but are the dogs—how many of their departures do we still suffer under a different name or delusion—the need for reward, the calamity of competition, retribution; in the morning light the tamp of plastic awning and in the evening clack of roof tile, the living we divine by *imagining*.

We waited at the train station while, in fact, she would arrive a day later. At eight, in the rain, and again at ten, after dinner, with the abundant clouds parting for a few stars or airplanes, we kidded each other by the tracks. The following night would be clear and return to us a thousandfold stars who had been gone it seemed much longer; and be fiery even by day, and near to us as if just behind the blue canopy we held up like a lung completely filled with air. A light world, rising and falling slowly like heat and temperature, with the considered movement of an insect, unthoughtful, intuitive, for which these stars chose their nearest kin and sent her, radiant, to every surface, even to the window where she took me by surprise, the hair, eyes and teeth of being taken. A day later it would be the familiar mistral throwing salt from the sea miles away over a shoulder for luck, tumbling leaves like chances; no less unpredictable because familiar.

I finished yesterday the whites—now lindens shower sunshine on bright forms, their outline blowing on the line blurred by mistral and, fooled as by destiny, I place in them trust, human increments for all they imperfect: elbow-wear and, black-edged in the purple fold, a small round hole before the ash sank whitely to the flesh where, cold, she didn't feel it, half-curled, half-thrust into her custom blond guitar, jade inlay marking for her gray-green eyes a mood's stops and frets. A bottleneck thrums the electric strings to violin or steely bass—amplified, ectoplasmic, serenity and serenade diffuse and would be treason to satellite and underwater lines agog with murder. Were she not so young, she would be a graft, publicized along those lines, to the pope's, the president's, shot-filled member. She calls men fingers digging and burying in the palm, petroleum blood, and systematically eschews their meat and grammar, summery acanthine in madness of when.

In the film version she writes across his forehead in lipstick MINE. We drank cool liquid out of Chinese decanters at the villa under its long beams, under the overfed moon. We kept the inside cool like a cave and, very sober, waltzed to Vivaldi, missing the minor tones. I took her on the white wool rug protecting cold stone, two unmodified extremes, black and white marble. We were interrupted by a family, a husband and wife and wife's mother, to whom the house was to be shown. Had they not seemed tranquilized we could never have avoided being in the same room together sharing one blouse. Having come to say good-bye properly, the other, different and equally undemanding, never even saw the inside of the house. She drank three glasses of milk on the back veranda, peeling the croissant crust off the chocolate bread, and asked us to lie in the grass. For once the sun was directly overhead, neither casting shadow nor, where it did make shade of the overhang or leaves, distorting their proportions. We were one mouth unadorned, making an imprint. As lithographic ink is black before it is receptive to any other color, the most moving operation is that of the almost complete effacement of the first imprint.

The essential is an undifferentiated mass from the unconscious cataract that acts by mesmerizing and at the same time loving us into relationship with the conscious. The most uncomfortable remark, myself, and yet the kernel of all jealousy is, at the same time, the ally. So many things to get done to do nothing. Fighting a few insects out of a hole, the present tense with cerebellum and suggestion. Without the eyes of instrument, without the eyes of involvement. Sitting all day next to a hardened shit, so what? To place your own indifference next to nature's, the pink amoral stone, to hold a whole all at once like a lover. Early sex, iris, eucalyptus outside the Song of Songs. Good night's sleep, that rarity when the pleasure of love-making lasts for days, a lighter vessel: power is its calamity. Fairness, gentleness, an example like a table, cloth in place, clean silverware, glasses with lemon waiting for cool water—the bay side. Valuable to meet you inalienate at your center where you are as yet unformed. Sorry to be so blunt about it. Happiness is funny, everything so delicately balanced and hiding because it's perfect. The herons say good-bye as they rush off somewhere unknown but alluring. To keep their hearts from breaking they say good-bye carelessly without looking back. Born to sing

> *Do not come back. If you can bear it, be . . .*
> *as the farthest sometimes helps: in me.*

The black cows of these mountains, the Labrador's black ridge against the door, its scorpion knob blackly luminous as through tortoise shell, sienna, sorrel, lacquer, back-to-back lust and insomnia, ferment and black-filled pap, white night, its little death unmanned, clings to the suckspot, black bellybutton death, feasible pause and, cranky for wishing it, wishing it, a war memorial, chaste and inflicted on simple earth, its lot of materials twisting a tongue out of all night of funk. *A dieu* soft garden, fingernail-lining silicate, promised hypnotic, salt of a heartlike plant in a green plantation, turning your radar acreage stalk or limb in the black unison of sleep due east, let go the silhouette dagger.

Third Epitaph

Under the black leaves of the laurels, the amorous
flowers of the rose, here have I lain who knew to comb
verse on verse and make a kiss flower.

I grew up in the land of nymphs; I lived on the island
of women friends; I died on the Cyprian island. This is
why my name is illustrious and my column annointed with oil.

Do not cry, you who stop: I was given a beautiful
funeral; the female mourners tore their cheeks; they put
my mirrors and necklaces in my tomb.

And now, on the pale prairies of asphodel, I promenade,
impalpable shadow, and the memory of my terrestrial life
is my subterranean joy.

The very perfume Kienholtz must have used in his environments on the 1950's—the slow music, the polyurethane men at the bar, or servicemen in the waiting room of a house of prostitution, memorabilia about Eisenhower—all on a brown and red carpet of roses. Your mother's letters at your bedside table, unopened, overpower the wilting cherry reds. She follows you to Europe with her drawl and plaint. I practice the flute, cascading cheerful melodies with low notes on the end. The Festival, the tinsel, the flash of light in the eyes of the well known and us, driven into the event by your departure. That day we heard of the terrorism and shootings and were sorry we had believed you were going for a rest. Not that you would be involved, but that once there would find consort among those wronged. We surfaced among costumes on the promenade, the faces of the hotels marking a period of history when architecture was sculpture: colomnade and white facings below black ivory domes, crystal high in the dining rooms' omphalos. We drank Samboca under the celebrated sky, blacker and more riddled for your absence. It was your drink, and we sipped to the hard coffee bean, split like a nipple; we were surprised— very few people had heard of it, although it is not uncommon.

Her first few times had been in parents' cars and even with a few parents, but mostly with boys a few years older—and better than their fathers. Girls talked about her and imitated her speech without knowing it. Teachers put her in front or in back of the room depending on their openness to sport, for she understood clearly the despondency of a high school education and of its educators and played upon their broken fields; or, rather, behind them—where the tall hedges met the low wall. Intimate with self-knowledge, she knew what to like and what was all right to like and liked confusing the two. And she liked two at once—though it would be years before boys became man enough to see themselves in other men. She was healthy because she was careful because, free of guilt, she often chose the hand over the heart, specifically, over the pants, clean, quick. When the police pulled up with their hard rubber flashlights banging the window, her clothes were in evidence on her instead of against her. Animal, vegetable, mineral: the sun is probably shining over her now in a convertible. She would tell a lot of women where to get off; some knew what she meant.

Like a cousin who fell from a horse, the weather changed suddenly, thrown into mistral. One of you went away, the other inside herself, from whose window a face shone, but shaded. I walked many hours each day without pleasure, like jogging, because the exercise was good for someone I might want to be later. The morning jasmine, dogs, kids skating too fast or falling, materialized slowly like dampness from stone rained on in the night. By four in the afternoon, perhaps, a clear thought; or a stone from the morning walk remembered like a hard decision, its cold beauty there on the strewn path. Too many birds, singing. From the other side of the valley a tractor engine, heard when I concentrated. A tight muscle, petals heated in the suddenly too hot sun drooping, behind a sealed window a slammed door—windwheel, will o'wind. Giving in—to the thousand dizzying steps you might take in a different direction; and you other, taking them into your room and mounting them in a narrowing perspective away—I bury a cry in the jowls of the wind.

A cry comes out and is the changing exterior, particles without apparent cause in threes who vanish without a trace. Here and there and where, moebius space. Who heard suck, who sucked? In the heaven of intuition, a network of pearls where one reflects, where one reflects all others, transient appearances are made. They are made without choice and catch in the netting below or fall through but as through space without gravity, the famous and unexplored falling-not-down. How long they hold there or are absolute elsewhere changes in timeless pandemonium. No one notices probably; probably notices no one. The sea in the distance is now pulling the stars, in the distance at any time and at will, awry as sparkles on the water. What matter! The perfect thing for you here. World polite as it collides, as it surprises. Assume the simplicity of the lattice: in our alternative *or* became *and*. And how! How can two of anything communicate so quickly, carried from one place to another like a light-wave for all it seems instantaneous. I seem to see. Therefore under the blue lights rests a girl with a fan and her dress tied under her breasts. She is large, filling half a large chair, looking ahead at herself discreet. Impossible to imagine her not there. The intoxication of the mind is the matter with the body. Colors are outlines with special effect unforeseeable—scarves, capes, nightgowns willing the wind to arrive, imported curtains to part. And one evening half asleep like a drug also arrives, late, making signs like a crazy person, a violin by itself. So the poppies out of the stone are drawn, curious, to love as to fresh air, waving, aware, complimentary, waking the sun.

The hundreds of leaves inside our dreams also quiver, they quiver, believe it. Like a range of mountains, out of hearing they are earth visited. Bay-leafed, the hands we hold. And on them the maps crossing from right to left, beginning to end. Bodies sequestered into souls. When they are laments we hear them as if they are immersed in water, blurred with tears. And as blessings, if at all. No doubt where I walked as a child, razing the air. If we dare, if we are the cage we painted with an open door, one of the many like a touch of dust in sun accidentally fells the outline with its colored chalk. Little tokens of myth, dream. On a stalk the water lily, on its spring the mushroom, such clamorings on the white pillow! Pass by. Because atop midnight like a scaffolding already we change our mind not sad together, interminably between, flower and fruit. The hexagram which forms RAIN in the sky falls as rain to sweeten the salt water. There we go swimming out in it at the ends of the polished fingers pointing at us, gradually merging into wave. Of the slender towers, gorges, beehives, hermitages, tumbling ranges, waterfields, the sea stradles the globe, more moon than earth, vicarious. One passes with a loaf of bread on her shoulder wrest from the burden of the sea, its great salt lips that search for mountain streams by squatting at the shore or throwing themselves like a discord upon it, familiar but elusive, one of the different women who invite you home as though there were such a place, as though such women find you. They do not become destiny. With their song of the sea, with their timepieces, their waterpipes, they are the hours of the day, the hours born in the alley, the hands taking the glass off the lamp and lighting it. The garlic and peppers hang from the ceiling. The honey and lemon, great nocturnal watches, gold pieces in the other life, whenever you wish. Not much different from advancing you will speak simply, one word in front of the unspoken.

She swam out in her see-through suit after I told her this story: he used to fish floating the flies and metallic pictures of worms, or real worms which he tied rather than pierced to the end of the line. He never used hooks. The nylon lay lightly on the water; he thought it was like a mating game because the lures were the same color as the trout, silver-blue, and sometimes with feathers, which he preferred because they were more buoyant. He bought the lightest nylon, the most delicate lures, so that there is the sharp image of him slowly pulling in the line as if pulling in the horizon, with the fish following once in a great while the long way to him submerged to the hip in his rubber boots, green like the lake algae. The algae were different in the higher elevations, oily and thin, and a kind of person was called to that place who would like to see through the water—the rest of them caught and ate their fish. Fish with fans iridescent and, unfortunately, irresistible. Sublime drop, as from mountain to sea, where she rolled her one-piece down after the fashion, shoring up all her hair with two pins, among the wealthy and not.

O restless one, who climbs to the top rung in the rain and slips on the last dowel, searching the far hills for morning in its yellow slicker; or, on the way home at the dinner hour, late autumn mulch smell in a gust with evening-roast, you take the wrong turn suddenly into a thicket; the stray dog there, his snap, and the eyes on a tree trunk with coarse brows; a creak; a cry, yours—covered with a quilt in your sleep like moon by fog—wrestling the hammer of the woodpecker out of its parody of your heart; and in a sweat throwing the cover off now, freezing the cat on the sill by dilating its gold eye with the one of yours whose door snaps mistakenly open on its crusted hinge. Sleep shapes the pillow of the weary and infirm, of the one woken by rain, and of the others in thought and in love, turning. A rise of late moon chafing the sky slips between earth and a few stars, perhaps the one you were dreaming of or, through a closed lid, projecting from; therefore the disc must be rolled away with an arm as if across a dark sheet. Inertia squares itself, yogic, and breaks you almost into consciousness to budge it, falls into the perimeter of the circle and tumbles in its moon finally away from you. Heavily the magma of earth's core shifts, throwing a few warm coals into your hands; and then, because you have sunk so far, rested, believed, you reach the fires kept burning. And burn your craft there, waking.

Women who fly on separate planes to meet in strange cities, poppies with their black follicled centers, chicken eggs with a little blood on the shell like a stain on a sheet, the stain soaked through and left on the bedpad unwashed, print housedresses washed and, in the wind, torn at the hem; pneumatic alliances: the plane too low, a drinking glass pitched off a table, uncracked, but with its blow to the head, unmarked, bleeding inside a drop; bird coo, too regular, parrot trained to the French national anthem, bumblebee, its lion markings burned black, stabbing the window and otherwise horrible fly. Brain dust, spindletops blown in the air, brow furrowed with electric violin practice, seeds planted too close in a furrow, tomorrow, because of a dream; giving orders; taking orders; the wearing of black, the wearing of mirrored glasses; dust; haze; ants on a naked woman, lipstick on a man; with a penknife, manipulation of a developing Polaroid; periodic rinsing through the night of the menstrual sponge; the days and the nights sulphuric between golden and leafy, between the sun and the moon: discharge, between flights in an airport: dizziness; black, yellow, red; yolk, ink; the beautiful striations after the sun sets invisible, as without love.

September of mother small and of animal, autumn of wood smoke. I was twenty-five, I had bought a cabin in the north in the tight hills. Maple and pine, and beyond, pine and oak, and behind, birch. I heard a sound in the woods as if it stopped for me, dog or bear, and when I woke, when I walked, I deferred. Waiting, feared, afraid, found nothing and knew the loneliness which is nothing, and started into recognition: a deer. And then the shot out of season, someone else's loneliness pinched into repercussion, the will demanding of the soul-off-guard and seizing its game. I ran into the deeper woods, the giving up getting over you, a liberty I had taken into the forest and gutted.

Sparklers from the July sky crease through the organdy and in autumn you burn again when the owner of the *bacal* at the corner raises your woolen skirt. The moment illumines a path through the crates of vegetables and fruit in the partial sunlight, the sacks of chestnut and raisin, to the window behind the counter where the sewing things lie on the sill, to pick a thread from the colored boxes that matches the fabric in your hand. You gasp, you exclaim, he withdraws, you buy the thread and mostly forget it until the year when, at home, you flush as a woman with what was thrust on you then, desire electromagnetic and adult, the massing of an arousal you couldn't possibly stop alone and yet, in the gravitational field of the village with its bakers and families of streets, did, which confused you. You do more yoga. You make yourself by posture and breath relax and lapse, taking from each what can rouse in you now a force to equal it easily, to come to discard it.

The greens grass, outburst toward the sky, the fig tree dances with Matisse as he cut himself out before dying in the shape of its leaf and the gorgona shape, curly-haired half-mermaid, half-weightless bird smaller and more precocious than the dove: *rossignol, hirondelle, mésange*; and somewhere the expensive alizarin streak a masquerade, *maquillage*, rouge on the body.

I alter nothing for her; that is how change sweeps me. Imagine the momentum of sea, how at the shore the pressure is realized in the slightest touch. Where there are pines and sea together I arrive in the present. The sea, the scar it makes each time it cuts the sand. Three smooth stones, their musical bodies in my hand. Turning, I turn them over. If we think, we aren't in motion. I stand and walk across the red tile and open the window by the center clasp. Each side goes out from me into the room. The rocker, the red lampshade, the two flutes and photographs of events, the French lilacs stolen. Their hair is ruffled, they've just gotten out of bed. I am the bird that flies out when they part. Each side goes out from me into the room, red hair, brown, the chiseled chins, sun and moon. When one is out I forget, I go into that one until the details are so great I recognize them in myself and can't remember where I am. April the almond tree, April the waterfall, April the first of summer, for summer then is a surprise. They wear each other's clothes, the red sweater that once was a guide, the white sweater and white shirt, white so different from white. Young, younger, youngest. The path to the olive grove, the grove, the black olives. Each of their mothers arrives, one takes her away and one takes her away. I have the time to myself, watermark where minerals once slept; jays tumble into dry rushes from the air. If I might complete a gesture on the flute, nothing can equal the radiant human element. Returning is a message. She invites me into her room. At last I'm alone.

The gods are never the same but remain the same body or rather the sign for it, hearts like pears like beacons. It was only a bird! skirting the salty bands of sea air. You flew. The small good-byes thank you but only because they are following. The large and the best, the ones who must duck to enter, the peaceful black squares asleep on their funny white circles, they will never stop you with surprise. You have an idea in four colors—on the indigo blue sea with a yellow ribbon around it, a fishing boat with red oars floating on the waves a spiral fishnet orange like hot coals. The smell permeates the whole memory, tickles and clucks and crackles as it comes in the small window, past and able to hurry you toward the beach with good humor. There you are, ever since childhood, that warmer country. As legend says nothing, you pick up the sounds and feel. Turn, the curly hairs waving in the south wind. Turn, the whistling. The plums falling on the fallen blossoms. Freshly whitewashed, the bases of the plane trees, minutes going by. And the flowers in the sand like spirits that close in daylight. Very rested, very smooth, all on the glassy surface patiently. Matter as instinct like eyes gleaming. Equally rare, this massless grace, beautiful white cloud I feel as a child in the blue sky, are the last made yesterday. They aren't personal, nor is one stone on top of the other a temple. The first days there are as one drunk, the vertigo of palaces and villas. The ravine in front inspires a sacrifice, but. Nerves ringing. No background. Riders flung. Eyelids lowered. Waves flash, being chosen. Not thinking, reverberating as eating and retiring for the night. A line is drawn like a tributary and in a circle a garland where, at the tops of trees, milk cools slowly in a footbath waiting for a guest. The symmetry of half-closed eyes along the line of bird flight, and the flags so sure of their movement. The mountain ranges fade that all day lowered bushels of light on prickly trails. I remember when the splendid mouth separates from land and sky, water again as I go out to meet the paired eyes of the fishingboat lights. Gleaming in their heads, sexual, tilt the whirlpool irises, off-centered dahlias, flowering scents confused at the hypotenuse of honeysuckle and mint. Making icons in their saffron and purple robes, in their monasteries, the flowers intend and imply. Beauty abandons the traversed latitudes—seven thousand and seven pagodas the work of people. When the faithful want to pray, when the prayer alights, it is dawn. And, extricable like yellow ochre from earth, when desire spills out of synch it finds you absent-mindedly spinning a globe, the bazaars, the exterior lives. Tin the boxes. Gold the rings. Nails, clocks, tobaccos, hashish in its powdered form, dust and cobble in theirs, green kohl, carved scarabs, silk, fringe, garlic, eggplant, chickens, leather, cooked meat, yoghurt, flatbreads, camels, mules, cows, sheep, dogs, parrots, canaries, chess games, old books, candelabra, paperweights, sandals, slippershoes, prayer rugs. Embedded, wedded, the stall to the hangings. Before the snakes are brought out, the northwest, you see how they will be. Called to, you and I. Isn't the other dazzling? I stood in the high sun looking down. In a shallow bowl lemon light pulled in the wind like a boat onto shore. No other pelago than this when nostalgia seeks a vessel. Tendencies to exist, details expressed, unusual features of the world like the spiral, place next to large public events private ones. Without thinking the meeting took place, prescient; as long as the well-known took to cross, longer was the anticipation, ethos large and in front of me aristocratic. All that I knew imagining went beyond. Churches and baths—churches out of sand and baths when the sea floods in. Beautiful arches like bodies in love and veins of darker sand leading to the water, labyrinthian, hold like cathedral light whatever I say after the fact: energetic mountains beauty tires of; therefore the miracle of the tide accepted. The hymns and the prayers fire, the rhymes air, they are cheering. Breath of god and with two unspeakables!

Four kinds of song, at least—sweet, insistent, erratic, shrill; and hare traversing the thorn bushes that would berry. Butterflies paired, almost clapping to their flutter; and the rustle of olive, pine and fig. So the porch overhanging the valley signaled the hours with its players. Time rounded into a sun who appeared to stand still, then flattened to the horizon, became measured and horizontal again like Euclid's geometry, explainable. Matter, at a perfect temperature, a certain mood, dematerializes before us, takes on more than its qualities and irrecognizable, we say it disappears. Love, calling itself into being. Or the dancing bear at the end of a pin—happy relative molecule. A haze of heat, an idea, a chance meeting, color. Made of mutually exclusive vibrations each with its unknown, its irreconcilable heartbeat, insect-whir. We traveled here and arrived after. We play a duet and don't hear it, hear it differently, hear it later, heard it somewhere before. The heat, the song fills us, therefore we say we are hungry, and we uproot the lettuce at dusk. "Lettuce," "dusk"—they mean something and are funny, a sort of a song.

She left the party saying I should drop over, which I heard an hour later. It was on my way home, barely, but because of the road I took, exactly. The light was off, which should have been enough, except a candle shook a circle onto one wall. I said I was sorry to stop by so late, and indeed was; we drank and I watched her drink, pouring that slow Southern voice. She took the stem with two long fingertips and thumb, twirled it like a cliché, and laughed. She held the glass and our laugh and our few hours up to the light and we saw them and tumbled them darkly about the room. She pulled and I buried my face in her so I wouldn't hear or heard other, through the tall grass and moonlight I made of her hair and eyes. I was there because I separated my eroticism from love; in love, sometimes I was erotic, through a chink where I flew out of time; but where I didn't belong there was never time, and I hoisted myself onto its smooth back, broke and disappeared and recollected myself, and left. I stood on the night porch with my shoes off, feeling the cool painted boards, golden under the rural street lamp. Night tossed back its head and a star fell, slowly and then suddenly into the far fields, like a look someone gives, anonymous, and touching in a distant fecund place. The car was a cool animal in a night I didn't have to look directly at nor speak to but who understood I was grateful to be passing through and, through, home and, home, that he was asleep, whom I almost desired.

It's a precise preference, the panorama divulging its inner trigrams duration and grace, unequal and absolute. Adding silica to these minerals obtains a *cristal* free of molecular angularity, known to the Chinese as exhaustion-of-the-masculine, such its clarity their book of wisdom places it at its close, torture and eros before completion.

She whispered *anemones* naming the flowers the boy had brought, a minor scene against the erotic masterpiece of the girl and her older lover Brando. We walked in in time for and accentuating the suddenness of their first intimacy in an unfurnished apartment. Driving home, after the movie, people we passed almost knew what they were doing in the back. The sunroof was open on the powdery sky and the narcissus from Tangiers smelled differently on each. One wore it like a light laugh surprising the air, the other like a vapor. I drove carefully exercising my hearing—I loved to hear first and see later and later still to touch. Taste, the darling of life, lay on her rosy couch on the other side of arrival, where we would fall as into a great beginning elsewhere, after acceleration, after light and sound. First it was like talc and then oily. I let myself take in from the back a finger, and there the darkness of all our colors lacing the room quickly magnetized in one spot like absence focused upon and enlarged—light, lightly. I was disappeared into an impersonal moment where the casual is sacrosanct; that anemone, for example, into which I was driven and from whose center I was pulled, into time, rested, ready to sleep.

Thirty mirrors ranged round its periphery, each tilted slightly from the next. The images cast by the mirror-drum as it revolves pass over three apertures so arranged that each gesture explores one-third of each image. Behind these apertures are three photoelectric cells, connected to the necessary amplifying equipment. At the receiving station the currents enter three neon tubes. The light from them is focused by means of a lens upon a revolving drum, similar to that at the transmitting station, the light being thus reflected upon a translucent screen. Two black and white goats running into their full three-dimensional image where the high rock meets the low-hanging limbs, a view of the opposite hills. What a few days of transparency would do. You keep pulling fibers out, distracted by birds. Fish-shaped flowers and bird-shaped leaves. Blessed again, wrong again, even measure, that relaxed vocal style, the gender of deities. Polyphony appears feminine. Slowly and seriously the petals falling down, a little schoolgirl madness in their trampled gowns. Slips. Gnats, wasps, calla lilies, a woman drawing her lover on the grass. The grass! Spring risks. The lover making the gigantic trust with and without knowing. Everything else is fantasy, peace sans form. Anger, resentment, bitterness, rage, displays of temper profile when you play.

Domesticity

Four slaves guard my house: two robust Thracians at
my door, a Sicilian in my kitchen, a Phrygian docile and
mute to serve me at my bed.

The two Thracians are beautiful. They have a club in hand
to chase away poor lovers and a hammer to fix on the wall
ornaments sent me.

The Sicilian is a rare cook; I paid her twelve *mines*.
No one else knows like she does how to prepare fried
croquettes and opium sweets.

The Phrygian bathes me, combs and depilates me. She
sleeps in my room in the morning and during three nights,
each month, replaces me next to my lovers.

They met at ten and in our twenties they opened a friendship to me of playfulness and calm. I loved their love the few times I left the house to them, the few I stayed and watched their summery second-nature expand to several days. I answered phones, suggested meals, happy to lend their intimate absorption a neutral body. They fed each other from their plates in restaurants with the invisibility of a neutral gesture—neither bourgeois nor sophisticate saw the tall man caress his friend's red beard in mid-sentence. His cock too seemed lathed out of some redwood. As if it had seduced the carpenter's hand into leaning against its delicate grain it leaned, sensibly, to the right, the rare coincidence of our pleasure. Female and male converging on a spot so tangible the other in his sleep rose, pale sundial in the Sahara-colored light. I kissed it sitting where I was until he woke and flushed the tip quick purple—and hung there between them and was their lief.

The best jump lightly into the air and lift more lightly before landing. The brashness of the American choreographer to let speak one by one his inarticulate troupe. When I observed your practice sessions against your will with their odors of wool sock and their eight a.m. rays gilding the Erik Satie, the three-minute Satie repeating, repeating, you landed as lightly as you rose. To do something over and over even if it's wrong, especially if it's wrong, one must be alone or without ego. Black leotard, yellow and green wools. The sweat rolling under the piano. Driving the coast road years before in a starless moisture, sixty m.p.h., my lover and I swerved around a black heifer crossing the stripe, blackening the night in heavy clef. He said the heifer could have taken the Volkswagen in the gut and us. I saw out of the corner of my eye its eye. On the quiet ride the rest of the way I knew I would leave him, the way I left you, cautiously, unceremoniously. To walk out into the high grass and piss on the spot and beat the sun down the horizon. The night has its eye, which I mistook for closed, and then for a mirror, and then for a friend. When I make love all night I remember the color: always the green of the Mediterranean far back in time, the shade bronze turns in brine or piss. The curtain is green, it rises and no one thinks it is pulled.

I have some snapshots of this coat over the years, up to today when it unraveled, its ribbing caught on the rose thorns outside the countess's door. In the negative the luminous thread repeats the outline of the oriental cherry she planted soon after moving to the south of France and which chokes the anonymous local fruit tree with bloom. The coat is from Hong Kong, hand-embroidered with the same tree, and I wonder if she will take it with her to Barcelona along with my camera. She is now up posing the countess, where it must be difficult for her to achieve a natural countenance as each feels the slight of the offer reneged upon for dinner. She's going to have it difficult where she normally has it easy, as the countess is jerked back from senility by anger and demands much more coherence from her than she, in the drugged mood she prefers to work in, inclines to. In her absence I watch the rain pool on the porch like the concentric abandon of a delightful idea when it occurs in a mind able to follow it without regard to time until it becomes simple. The hours of rubbing graphite on stone, the lifting of the stone from bench to press, the inking of the block and the cleaning of the ink, the application of the tusche, the moistening and sizing of the paper, the registration marks . . . The David Hockney print she sent from London in Chinese blue and white called "Rain" mocks my abbreviated days with its long process, his leisure to invent after that period a process for merging paper-making and paint, where he dropped in for a visit and stayed a year.

Lead weights sewn in the hem to keep it down. The fitting over, the pleated, cross-stitched dress came off in halves and was arranged by a younger girl on the dummy. In high heels and underwear before the child's permitted stare the client stood arguing with Andassa, the two great chests firm and their voices low. Andassa yes-madamed her and got her way, the covered buttons, the price. The woman disappeared in her purse and brown suit. The child found a weight among the needles and pins, the clippings on the floor, and bit it furtively. So soft a metal amused her despite the pinpricks on the hand when she was seen. The cat carried two kittens back to her litter from under the scraps, and the girls teased and laughed when the seamstress left the room to warm the milk. White Russian Andassa—her black and white tiles opened onto a terrace, whitewashed and bleached, that was our roof. Her girls hummed the last few hours every evening, late over some decoration, singing *under the table all my life among young women's thighs*, which I would repeat. They made me a *hanoum* outfit with gold-trimmed velvet bust and lira-edged veil. In his wallet a little photograph where he's kneeling, his hand a fan below my slave-girl lap.

What young girls do to jettison the heat, shake water from their hair, smoke, nervously pace the afternoon, can bore us. Seeking to enter it, like water sweated onto stone, they are baffled to residue, pollen or salt. The fig leaves unfurled in early May suggest acacia, suggesting to us the sunny beach behind the square whose hem of acacia was pierced by springs, uncurling like tendrils across the tile and asphalt, and the beach be a slip for our tired feet as we look for the large brass key by flash and starlight. The moon will rise from its pine its olive or its fig, letting the bird dart across, and the sky be a lilac brought close to the eye.

She was reading *Justine* that spring, and slowly, as she began to stop fantasizing the manner in which her success would come to her, understood Durrell marking insecurity a haunting quality. Slowly because unpracticed; carefully, in that she saw how even a great artist who postulates a narrator different from himself reveals a political faux pas; she knew Justine had been overly prized for her shrewdness—not by possessing it but by manipulating her lack. She was becoming the woman she wanted to know. Was proud; did not cling to it. Braided in the Swedish style her hair revealed a specific great beauty; circled by thick coils, she became surprisingly boyish; was not, was languid and controlled; passionate slowly like her reading, thorough, light. Under the fig tree, which gave out onto a ridge of pine and olive, you photographed her self-consciousness and then, finally, directly, her gaze, large, Mediterranean dark, blue. Without birds, without their whistling over the music of the creek, though she laughed like a flute none would have caught it, clung to it, played it back much later in other southern but never so fair, fair even but never so perfumed, countries.

The room shrunk in the July humidity and I surprised her specifically in the afternoon in its excess to disappear into the flattery she felt at my visit, a flattery that opened her pores and onto which she splashed a then popular European perfume. I still think of her when I see a glossy of the bottle in *Vogue*. She was easy to be around and made me forget my other entanglements; like strong perfume she overcame their presence. At the time she worked odd hours to save for the expenses she imagined incurring later. Having passed a number of examinations with honors and chosen to neglect those honors, she knew only that she would leave the rural plains of her youth and need money, first because those who would be willing to provide for her were those to avoid, and later that to those whom she wanted she must prove it was an unnecessary formality. The fan shook and hummed and is the sound for me now when I think of that region, the gnats and mosquitos accompanying its manured fields, along which I would drive after. She liked to climb quickly and be there first. And slower in the back room among the coats, suddenly, under her black skirt, easing the leotard astride my wrist. But in the summer she fell back onto the bed where we came over and over to tangle ourselves without mercy, she in my plans for leaving the following autumn, and I in her long legs, white body of summer; and in winter—where having to be clandestine was more difficult—whiter, less floral, except at her lips which were always rose-fair, rose-large, cavernous like the couch she first sat on at the party where we met, in a parlor under the fair shade of her hair.

On the mountain we'd sleep in the heavy shade—green figs like testicles and the leaf palms cracking with pungent milk—deliberately, having been told of the vaporous harm to the dreamer. Donkeys shifting their fly-besieged, sundazed gaze met and held ours; the goats would stop because of the short hobble they bore, their slitted eyes in suggestive succession fixing us blackly every few feet of film, those stills of them every few feet of hill annointed now as if memory were a kind of solution. We pile rocks on our bodies partly unearthed and sweat the weight wet. The air is still and imagining it through the labyrinth of rock and moisture against the skin in a breeze stiffens the nipple. Starfish, colossal under mounds seen from above, the bleached soft-colored rocks look too much like breasts, and the trouble you took for the angle and height makes it obvious. We get up heavy with stone shadow, each muscle rising like sea-cow, and fall into the green cove, afloat like the three tomatoes we cool and swim around, lazily pushing one back if it should stray, too intimate now you said to eat for lunch, so you sucked on the salty skin, you did, even though you were posing. Then there are mermaids, and other riffraff and dross.

From the hotel's sixth floor the print umbrellas—red dotted, turquoise, lemon yellows—arched their springy tops in the sun; like hats doffed in the wind they tipped; connected as if by cartilage, curved. And the linen whites sparkled translucent by the water, watery. After the long drive a late swim. By dusk we were upstairs with the view. An hour on our backs in the warm sea, stretching ankles to arches to toes, back overhead to the fingertips, and the whole body dolphinlike, bellied out, expressed. A chortle or two, a beer or two, a kiss, a sort of a sigh, a splash, a shower, a mock struggle, a tiny rose—out of order, the hours after arrival—disorder: the open grins of the suitcases, the damp towel over the lamp, starlight left in the rug kicked up where we kicked off our shoes; spare change left in the bed, cold to the cold ass; early to late dusk, two hours out of eternity's thin gold spiral that we knotted, bit, that you lay under your spine and floated on, that we undid and were naked on the sheets. And also slept there; woke at eleven, one by one the missing hours becoming clothes we found on the armchair, dressed, and had midnight for dinner.

Remember how close we sat in Sifnos having dinner by the water? You said in your country once you put the table *in* the water. You began the meal, and then what a great idea to move it over a little, it would cool you, it was that calm. You rolled your pants to the knee and poured drinks all around, the fishbones back to the sea. Lizards climb the stone outside the kitchen by the sea. Weeds and flowers grow out of the stone; the relatives spill out of the kitchen. The daughter is well educated or about to be. She serves us with the happy face of one who is leaving. You lifted your skirt walking home in the dark over the pebbles to sit. One night we saw the only other lovers—they were both fair, she blond and he gray—and their eyes moved only to each other and the sea, these two destinations. Now the sea once in a while slips a wave up to their feet, because a boat passes or for no reason, now the yellow moon divides the sea into fields.

They drove to the far side of the island. It was rocky and off-season. They found a house with a climb to the bay, and whose nights were protected by its gentle curve. From halfway up they would turn to the taverna lights casting out a short distance to water momentarily released from its journey under fishing boats, whose lights in the stillness went out of round where they entered it. By midday the vendor cries along the streets quieted and the fish was bought and cooked. One lemon to flavor the fish and squirt on the hands to clean. Goats feast on the rind. Bells on the goats in the heat, in the heat bells from the churches. Side by side they flattened out in the sun. Like a sheet in the sun is disinfected, they were, and were lovers who liked each other reduced to very few needs—mosquito netting, a white shirt, a simple meal, rhododendron and thyme steaming in a thicket by the path. They passed it like a gate between the house and the village. The pails with milk hardening into cheese in the cooler part of the house, so round and white, the opening of the well, the late moon—illuminations that come to them in the night, and why.

If we were as ferries and lived only a summer, how lovely to sleep without contact or mediary at the extremes of puberty, the rifling of the beaches where the cheerful oriole names the black walnut black gum, briar, hickory, white ash. Children spill out of the sexual like flags. One's a goat and one's a sheep. They belong to how fast horns grow, the over-ebullience of the overturned. Like a lyre or a flute made of eagle bone, the mistral. All appear from one and the same place, elegance, repose informed by choice. Nothing can be harmed in which a sneeze interrupts a dialectic: the darkening sky under which we close in on reality. Therefore the path, though the sand is covered when you say good-bye and turn to go. The reason for toleration rolls to the edge of the water in some mood. Birds in radio frequency, beasts of space who cast about for intrigue, a lovers' misunderstanding that lights the sky first thing. Solarized photo, shy moment in yellow. The pace alone has significance: the artist accompanies herself on a tin pan while the rosebush speaks to its generosity, getting slowly drunk. By the way, by the sea, by the word wait! having its last say. A monkey's remarks among which we arrange our air-mattress and lie down for a few hours in the sun, speculating on death-by-longing. The tail of the resentful leads to your door, the trail of the uneventful gets lost half a mile from how a leap is made love. And not taut, not worse, not first, the mortal moment of salt caked to the sides of boats, one or two kind acts.

Serenity's Walk, for which one takes a shower and is dried by the wind. The delicate reentry, like a spacecraft that must guide as through the eye of a needle through uncomfortable heat and pressure constraints, one must return to the conscious world. One sees the spectacular sunrise peripherally and hears the last of a silence. The body steps the earth as if feeling the curve, where last night it was driven to the edge of a sea, elastic, given up to sands. Gravel spongy with rain, countryside shifting intact upon its water table: the great canal, waking, oscillates. And the shimmer passes surreptitiously onto the *other*: flower, pine, lover. Waking as well from seahorse to groundswell to dew. Slowed to open; threshold of that-which-will-happen; place of sighs. The air moves and is a bird. Then the bird is a question and resolve, mind at play. Hair, weight, proportion, primary colors, the verifiable third dimension—the friendly threes—settle into their solids, their attachments, beginning. Simultaneity, like breakfast on a silver tray, oval-, crescent-, heart-shaped. One eats, one smells, one feels: reunion.

Melons best and then berries. A city where anything was obtainable and people loved, because each had come from somewhere else, a variety in which they were represented: linen, silk, good cotton, and how these steamed in our salt in summer. The cry of the vendor, dry, foreign, announcing, on the last of the vegetable trucks, reptilian cauliflower, beans, and the powdery peaches whose undersides held the shade of the Negro hands which had cooled them in the distant South; creaked down the burning street, this mechanical horse, and was unburdened. Rubber, asphalt, concrete, stone, wrought iron, brick, the substances first introduced to a child as color—sienna, mahoghany, Indian, red oxide, blood, vermilion, carrot—and then as solids, the verticals and horizontals, the flat and the stub one bruises against. The tunnel to the park, its cosmic fluorescent; the park's climbed trees, the secret hiding place in a small boy's neck: tunnel and tree and humidity. Mother lifting the moon out of its brown-paper sky and easing the knife through it; and the knife wet with the small hairs of the central sponges—but airier than sponge, like the pliant night sky with its air holes of star—and the light would break the honeydew open at the last second so the two halves rocked on their ocean floor. The juice shimmered as the child balanced on the side and gazed into it as into a swimming pool. Sweet there and safe; cool. Four asleep in the one bedroom where the air conditioner beat. The floor all bed, the sheets ironed with a cool palm, the palm on my back rocking me in my sea-body.

Like the flesh of Venus is mud, every day is a good amount of time, and of purity beneath every irony, music without ambition, air. How deaf the life of the eyes. Three patches of sunlight in time. The bridge between past and present is that conflagration—first turn! The wind blows the rain off the leaves in the light. Big mind falling into place. How to leave behind one's etc., bold relief. Beautifully muscular, slight belly, milk overflowing stockings at the foot of the bed: Paradiso. I catch myself not breathing; what am I dying to change? The slightest noise makes my heart start. Voice the wide arenas with fruit trees, voice the comfrey and mint, voice the twentyfirst of August, voice under the sign of the fool, voice the gods in the hedgerows, voice a hammock, voice in a long-haired rug, voice your father's village, voice depth and serenity made present aster, onions, voice the steaming rice, voice circle of stones, voice wholly one over. What was the passage of the woman carrying eggs across the beach? Dressed in black with a sac on her back, from the bamboo stalks rickety stack. Plastic sac, glutinous, opaque, ovum of night, prehensile her, carapacean, nomadic, wearing slippers over the hot white rocks toward the promontory. A boy rolls a hoop across her path. Old in a cone of light. The hoop wobbles in its mirrored ellipse. It dips into the heat distortion rising from the rock and is saved by the boy with a stick. She shrinks as she walks into the shimmering cushion of air, framed by o-vaults of the passing hoop.

One biked easily to the gardens because the hills dipped musically. Tiered in colors, each rose possessed a magical name and the names in a foreign language. A stadium of flowers, each a rose. *Not to speak about roses, nor the moon. Nor the names of lost loves, common songs, nor odors, which cannot be recalled.* We sat on the edge of a bench, bent toward the gold light deepening the red bridge. The lights came on along the bridge and bronzed the bay below. When the light reached the roses it was divided into its individual chords, and each allowed itself to be touched where it was tired. We had to sit there because the light had gone out in our pockets and we were heavy with the light. You were gone as suddenly, and when I had the news two days later, the rain that was to ruin the soil and be unavailable the following autumn during the eucalyptus fires had begun. The smell of dung and menthol and mulched leaf dizzied like too much rain. Hundreds of acres of fire into tarlike sap. A friend, when you are not yet both twenty-one but close, breathes in the darkness that you might breathe in and flower. I sat on a bench in the rain on and off for days until the roses in that part of the country for that time of year burned with scent. I must have been, as I remembered it later, taking a bath during your last hour, in the house you had found for me on that decent avenue I couldn't afford. It was fair in those days to die rather than go back. Whereas today it is merely sunny, somewhat on the cool side; the village reeks of fresh bread.

They would send her to a hotel in Barcelona if she couldn't stop her moods. Anyway she spoke Spanish, with the good humor of one who has also studied Chinese, with a flair for its pictorial and lyrical quality. The contemporary version of her love of the classical guitar was the jade-inlaid electric she got in Hong Kong during a brief port of call. She was on the boat as a last attempt by her family to purchase her education; therefore the world. She was seeing it through the eyes of kif, those pearls that made her blue eyes gray. She carried her perfume with her like a veil, lacing her scent with American designer kitsch that, mingled with her skin, turned floral and impregnable. She attracted attention even when she was too inexperienced to notice and fail to dispel it, which she later learned by observing others do badly. With a languid mouth and quick step she would fly across the room and smoke with her back turned: a habit of hiding her nerves behind a blank expression that made her look younger and would be good for at most another year; already it was incongruous with the abstract beauty of her face filling out rose white, and rose red where the small scar on her upper lip drew a shadow. Before their car was found by the police she searched the old city in the deep purple hue of her jacket and of the dusk it never failed to signal and illumine where she hurried. By the sea at this hour she heard the song that eventually made her famous dimly chorused in the waves, in the underwater of the mind darkly, purposefully. She hitched home by the coast route to find them in bed, back from the police, annoyed at having had to leave their address. I was happy to slip the curtain of the street from her, the intoxication of her future made more palpable by her failure, which afforded her distraction, resolution and charm. She gave us half a sweet laugh, the half that is at herself.

Against a sky that would darken minorly in the small hours like a child not quite convinced of the nap and going deep and briefly asleep, I drove slowly scaling the notes of darkness and of her sleep in the backseat, child really, at twenty, down into pearl that became fog and mist in a wash of sunrise, to whom I had looked for that great centrifugal flare to boost me into other-worldliness, arrival. Sunrise was insubstantial, in fact, and raw and, familiar throughout the night, mere. She woke cranky. And would take, like the inevitable turning of a globe, her time, fractional to her, years to me, burning through to beauty. Hope is wine-red where first there is blood, leonine. Meanwhile, bloodshot, I got into the wrong bed.

Bleat of white goats, ruth of wind, pooled water. She is everywhere like the focal one disappearing. Heat flash into the phenomenal world. Contrariety is the play of god. Negations with blue eyes. The spiritual become spatial. Cave rain from the awning sky with the elegance of far-away birds, leaks, drifts, slips, rends. The furrows in your brow loosen the face and the other. Stop, slow curve, yield. Breath of bells long after your luminous eyes like that which flies away with memory. The arrogant morning red like tomatoes who could crack an egg on its nose and eat it raw later enters your hallway with candles. The sky, the heat, the very brim of the hat. Who has caught on? One is odd and two is odd as each is separate. And three is odd and four reduces to three and five is odd. Where are the elements who swore they were my mother? Their almond-eyed word whispers along a sun-scarred plain. You open through a green door; a tree opens into olives. This is the beach you're on that insists on smelling of cinnamon and an odd silver texture on the icon face. The cross persists as an instrument of torture, losing faith like boiling water its condition. Some few final jokes and the smell of lilac are windows that keep opening and exciting. If it's all the same to you, the air-lift pausing and rocking falls asleep and the feeling of seeing family from the mound disappears.

They only touch us and rise before us and stir the air into scent. They make perfume here in three stages: water and flowers are brought to a boil in a still; condensed water and essence are tapped into a Florentine vase where they separate owing to differences in density. Then, during enfleurage, each day fresh flowers are laid on a mixture of fat; the fatty materials become impregnated with perfume. At the end of the season the fat is kneaded with alcohol which brings out the fragrance. Finally, using a solvent which evaporates, the perfume is extracted from the flower: jasmine, mimosa, lavender, orange. Their cocks disappear in their leotards. The stars of the French ballet are Russian, extracted like teeth. The one in the front gives us his best smile; your aunt knew his teacher in Egypt. There's no way around, you forget. The hedges here are trained into position with coarse wire, then the lilacs dip playfully over them.

A fragment begins like melt the solid. A hundred or more fears and reveries, pregnant women, spring thresholds, start their stories. The rainmaker also chooses tales like picking berries. We hear, we are included. Whether the branches creak or green wood smokes crossing and uncrossing like legs the many roots we sit on, natural and magical gases suspend us like curious planets, like sacred cows whose milk and butter, sweet dung, grassy blossoms perpetuate the air around them. While listening, beached, while listening pressed between ferns, while sleeping, while offering, receiving. Why is the sky blue? Scattered wave light life centers. Spiral arms, thin sickles of other galaxies, don't contain our scattering dusts, the cries for joy. Nevertheless, how fast we listen for the more remote, the larger the shift. Daily survives, gushes into our universe. Reports, resources, songs, healings, codes on the red sky trail. Timpani! Marimbas! Chimes, beeps, hammerings, snares. We wheel, ritual work. The nerve of the universe is a fret. Vibrating orders: if you spear the dust from my eye, if you will and we make the large bed out of the dusts and feathers, out of this world, we alter discerning spirits. Whitecaps reach drifting down from the stars. When the winds settle they settle as favor striking its triangle among us, telescoping our differences; each time a side is struck the interior scrambles together. Never perfect and near-perfect bending, braving a direct look in one eye. Seen-through, each of us lessens a warp in space and continuum. Breaking the waves is a small thing, calm. A jug full of seahorses and the loss of faith with its secret red anemone confounding it—these at our feet as we look up as if that were a direction and not empowering. Snowflakes growing in the weightlessness of space? falling on a beach in the Aegean. Serendipity. We find, as when white light enters a prism or when sodium is excited, the odd miracle. A round object on earth, perhaps rolled away by someone, a straight line between people which they fear stepping on, the sphere appearing as a circle, abstract directions too opposite to meet, discover hope one cloudless revolution. From this turning, because of a sudden, certainties become probable. Pairs, night and day, our part of the world, and spin, dissolve into models, while over here alluding to experience without a hold are the twilights: the imperfect construct of heaven on earth letting, like a zephyr lets, go. Earth with a blush to its cheek, earth with a bell on its toe. The hills roll continent to continent, a mare with the virility of a horse and the devotion of a cow. Hills yielding grapes, almonds, apples, avocado, grains, spitting them forth in good weather or wrestling them loose. Water clings to the shallow places, modest drops of rain in union like geishas active and contemplative. They bend the grasses that return to feed. Within the earth the seedlings pantomine and on it the wild goose traces. All the lines the same, broken in the same vein. The only one that keeps is loving the earth, a concord of soil against loneliness, against intimidation the mountainous as-I-go, the watery hand of the Serengeti to hold. Black and green, standing or sitting harmoniously, carved as on a flat stone, vase or wall; or, walking embodied. Expressions of desire, amulets, yellow plains, reeds, and teeth of the wild beast. Trees in tribe arrange gifts, sunny days in a row, in excess and essential. And muds like whales, and frost, the dew of bears. The windy corners cough and rest and, especially being born, toss. The buoyant humor of fantasy is all we can do to keep ourselves in shape. Static electricities who have been massaged, we pick up intuitions like balloons. Green magnets in a blue frame with their addictions, their predilections, their repulsions as formless as numbers. Iconographic, pornographic.

Notes

Pages 5-6:   *periplum,*
> *not as land looks on a map*
>> *but as sea bord seen by men sailing*
>>> From Ezra Pound, *Pisan Cantos*, LIX

Pages 17, 20, 37, 59:
Translated from Pierre Louÿs, *Les Chansons de Bilitis*, Paris, 1894, and Monte Carlo, 1972.

Page 35:
Last two lines from Rainer Maria Rilke, "Requiem for a Friend," translated by Rika Lesser.

About the Authors

Olga Broumas is the author of five collections of poetry, including *Beginning With O*, which won the Yale Younger Poets Award, and, most recently, *Pastoral Jazz*. A founder of Freehand Inc., a learning community of women writers and photographers in Provincetown, Massachusetts, Broumas has taught at Goddard College and the universities of Idaho and Oregon. She has received a Guggenheim fellowship, a grant from the National Endowment for the Arts, and a Fulbright travel grant.. She is a graduate of the University of Pennsylvania (B.A. Architecture, 1970) and the University of Oregon (M.F.A., 1973). Her home is in Provincetown.

Jane Miller received a 1985 National Endowment for the Arts fellowship and has published two books of poetry, *Many Junipers, Heartbeats* and *The Greater Leisures*, a National Poetry Series selection. She is Visiting Poet at the University of Iowa, and has taught at Goddard College and at the Writer's Community in New York City. Miller is a graduate of Pennsylvania State University (B.A., 1970), California State University (M.A., 1975), and the University of Iowa (M.F.A., 1977).

About the Book

Black Holes, Black Stockings was composed in Garamond #3 by G&S Typesetters of Austin, Texas. It was printed on 60 lb. Warren's Sebago and bound by Kingsport Press of Kingsport, Tennessee. Dust jackets and covers were printed by New England Book Components of Hingham, Massachusetts. Design by Joyce Kachergis Book Design and Production of Bynum, North Carolina.

Wesleyan University Press, 1985.